16x/4/11/ 12/1

FAMOUS ARTISTS

VAN GOGH

The author, Andrew Hughes, is a writer, reviewer, and lecturer on art and art history.

Series design   Tessa Barwick
Designer   Tessa Barwick
Editor   Jen Green
Picture research Emma Krikler
Illustrators   Michaela Stewart
                  Tessa Barwick
                  David West

First edition for the United States, Canada, and the Philippines
published 1994 by Barron's Educational Series Inc.

Designed and produced by
Aladdin Books Ltd
28 Percy Street
London W1P 9FF

First published in
Great Britain in 1993 by
Watts Books
96 Leonard Street
London EC2A 4RH

All inquiries should be addressed to:
Barron's Educational Series Inc.
250 Wireless Boulevard
Hauppauge, New York 11788

Library of Congress Catalog Card No.: 94-14128

Hughes, Andrew.
Van Gogh / Andrew Hughes.
p. cm. (Famous artists)
"First published in Great Britain in 1993 by Watts Books"–T.p. verso.
Includes index.
ISBN 0-8120-6462-3 (hardcover).–ISBN 0-8120-1999-7 (pbk.).
[1. Gogh, Vincent van, 1853-1890. 2. Artists. 3. Painting, Dutch.
4. Painting, Modern–19th century–Netherlands. 5. Art appreciation.] I. Title.
ND653.G7H775   1994
759.9492–dc20
[B]   94-14128
CIP

International Standard Book No. 0-8120-6462-3 (hardcover)
                              0-8120-1999-7 (paperback)

Printed in Belgium
4567 4208 987654321

FAMOUS ARTISTS

VAN GOGH

ANDREW HUGHES

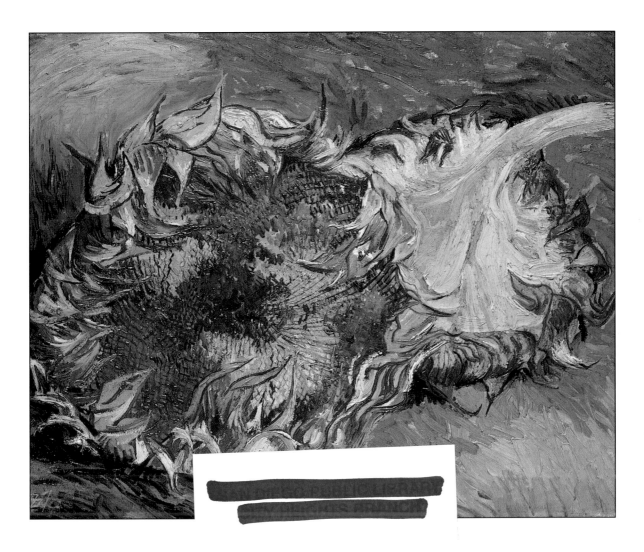

BARRON'S

CONTENTS

 The Starry Night, painted in 1889

INTRODUCTION

Throughout his life Vincent van Gogh was poor, often hungry, and ill. When he died in 1890 at the age of 37, it seemed that his work would be forgotten. All that has changed, and Vincent is now perhaps the most famous painter of all. In 1990 his painting "Dr. Gachet" was sold in New York for over $82 million, making it one of the most expensive pictures in the world. Van Gogh's paintings are colorful, bold, and passionate. Although painted 100 years ago they capture the world in a modern and exciting way. Yet this skill had to be learned and practiced. This book explores Vincent's development from beginner to great artist. It traces the story of his life and explains how major works came to be created. The artist's techniques are discussed, and you can try out some of the same methods. Below you can see how the book is organized.

An englargement of part of the painting

Illustration of the artist's home or environment

The story of the artist's life

About the artist's work at the time

The size of the paintings are indicated by these symbols.

A feature on the artist's technique with practical projects to try

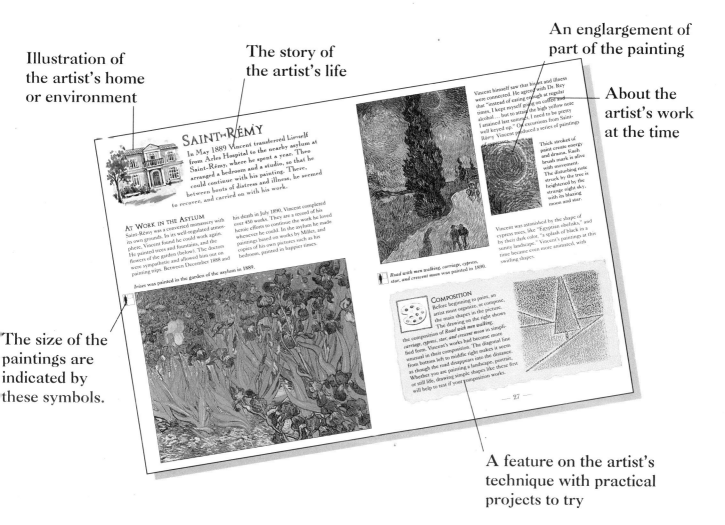

GROWING UP

Vincent van Gogh was born on March 30, 1853, in this house in Groot-Zundert, a small village in the south of the Netherlands. His father was a clergyman and his family were respectable, middle-class people. As he grew up, Vincent loved books and drawing but had no thought of being an artist until much later in life.

EARLY YEARS

Vincent had an ordinary, happy childhood. He was the oldest of six children, with three sisters and two brothers. He attended the village school in Groot-Zundert until he was 13. In 1864 he was sent to boarding school. Solitary and energetic, he was not a brilliant student.

Vincent became interested in paintings at an early age, partly because three of his uncles were art dealers. When he was 16, his Uncle Cent helped him to get a job in the Dutch capital, The Hague. He became a junior clerk for Goupil and Co., an important firm of art dealers.

GOUPIL AND CO.

Vincent spent six years working for Goupil and Co., surrounded by paintings, illustrations, and prints. The firm was impressed with Vincent, and in 1873, when he was 20, they sent him to work in their London gallery.

Vincent's brother Theo was also working for Goupil's, but in Brussels. The two began a correspondence that was to last all of Vincent's life. In all, almost 700 of Vincent's letters to Theo survive, often full of drawings. They are a wonderful record of the artist's hopes and fears, and the progress of his work.

Vincent is thought to have drawn this bridge near his home in 1862, when he was only nine years old.

When he was 11, Vincent gave this drawing to his father as a present.

CHILDHOOD DRAWINGS

Vincent's father and mother admired the careful accuracy of his work, and this was important to the boy. Drawing was also a way of recording the detail of the countryside where he loved to wander. Photographs were very rare at the time, so a favorite spot could only be captured with paper and pencil. The picture of the bridge that appears below left is so well drawn that people have doubted that Vincent did it at so young an age.

ENGLAND AND PARIS

In England, Vincent also learned some important lessons about life. He fell in love with Ursula Loyer, his landlady's daughter, and asked to marry her. She rejected him, and this upset Vincent very much. He was also distressed by the poverty he saw about him in London and the enormous contrast between the lives of rich and poor people. Vincent started reading the Bible and decided he wanted to help poor people. His work at Goupil's had been good at first, but now it began to suffer.

In 1875 Vincent was moved to the main gallery of Goupil and Co. in Paris. A year later, however, he was dismissed for being absent without permission. Vincent returned to England and worked as an unpaid assistant in a school near Hastings, and then in West London. His faith was becoming more and more important to him, and he began to preach sermons, in English, in the local church.

Milk jug, 1862

SKETCHING

A sketch is a quick drawing done for yourself. Get into the habit of carrying a sketchbook and pencils with you to record sights that interest you. Pencils have different leads. Those marked H are hard and sharp for detailed work. Those marked B are soft for blurry effects. An HB pencil is halfway between the two. See which you prefer. Practice making sketches, then try a detailed drawing like the one shown here.

FAILED PREACHER

By the age of 24, the religious part of Vincent's life had become so important that he decided to train as a priest. Returning to the Netherlands, he studied for three years, in Amsterdam and then in Brussels. On failing his church exams, he joined poor workers in a desolate mining area. Vincent slept on straw to help them and tell them about God.

RELIGIOUS STUDY

Studying to be a priest was, and still is, very demanding. Vincent had to study Latin and Greek as well as math, geography, public speaking, and of course theology. His father, Theodorus, was too poor to pay for this, but Vincent managed to persuade his uncles to sponsor him. Living in Amsterdam with his Uncle Johannes, he struggled for 15 months, working day and night, wearing himself out. In Amsterdam, at least, he saw Rembrandt's paintings and collected illustrations of his work.

WITH THE MINERS

Vincent failed to qualify for further religious study however, first in Amsterdam and then in Brussels. In the winter of 1878 he took a job as a preacher in the mine-fields of the Borinage in Belgium. It was a hard life that he deliberately made harder. He made sketches (above) and reported to Theo: "Most of the miners are thin and pale from fever; they look tired, weather-beaten and aged before their time." Vincent shared their life, ate and dressed as they did, and went down the mines to experience their work. But he put so much into his job that he alarmed his superiors, and in July 1879 he was dismissed for "irregular behavior."

Coal Shoveler, from the summer of 1879, a sketch of a working man

This drawing shows Vincent's sympathy for the miners, bent double beneath their loads. Even for lives as harsh as this, Vincent saw hope in religion, shown by the figure of Christ on the cross.

The Return of the Miners, in pen, ink, and watercolor, drawn in 1881, after Vincent had left the mines. This drawing is more sophisticated, showing Vincent's developing skills.

RECOVERY

Vincent continued to preach, living off his family. Without a home or job, he faced a crisis. Theo helped him, sending him money and drawing materials. Now Vincent wrote:

"I will take up my pencil, which I have forsaken in my discouragement, and I will go on with my drawing. From that moment everything has seemed transformed for me."

PEN AND WASH

Pen and ink drawings are lively and dramatic. Begin with a pencil sketch. Using a brush, create areas of "wash" with watered down ink or watercolor. Dilute part of the wash further to create a graded wash. Use a dip pen with a variety of nibs to make lines and marks of different kinds. You could also use a felt-tip pen. Outlines can be shaded in different ways, with lines like the ones shown here, or criss-cross marks like those in Vincent's drawing above.

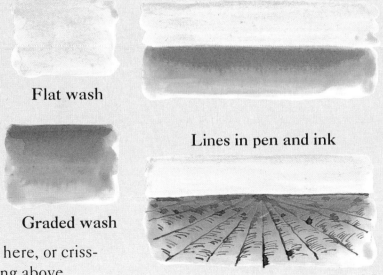

Flat wash

Graded wash

Lines in pen and ink

Peasant Painter

By the age of 27, Vincent had made the most important decision of his life, to become an artist. He spent the years between 1880 and 1885 developing his skills. He had little money and lived in cheap rooms all over the Netherlands, including the flat agricultural landscape of the Drenthe. There he drew country people. He was often ill and miserable, but determined to succeed in this new career.

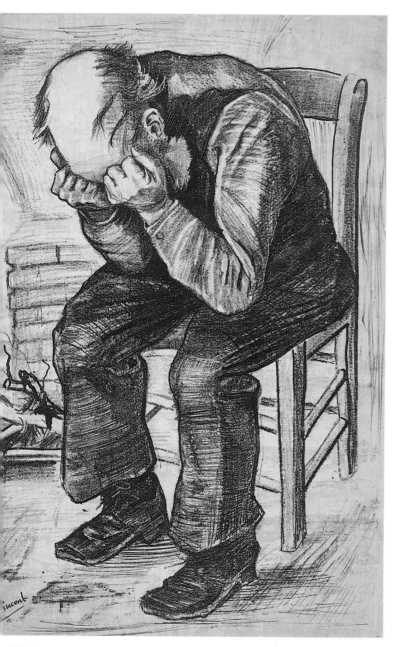

At Eternity's Gate, 1882. "I want to do drawings which touch some people," Vincent wrote.

First Lessons

After the failure of his studies for the priesthood, Vincent didn't want to study art formally at an academy. But he knew nothing of anatomy, the study of the human figure, or of perspective, by which artists show a sense of depth in work done on flat paper or canvas. Theo knew a rich young painter, Anthon van Rappard, who taught Vincent perspective, and lent him prints to copy. Vincent made hundreds of drawings of people, using charcoal, crayon, ink, and watercolor.

Learning the Trade

Vincent spent two years in Amsterdam and The Hague. He was given lessons in painting from the artist Anton Mauve, who was his cousin. Theo provided money for oil paint, and he began to paint in oils. Vincent often traveled to the country or the coast to draw working people. He was beginning to believe in himself as an artist, but he had little money. In 1882 he became so ill that he spent time in the hospital. In The Hague he made a home with Sien Hoornik, a local woman who had posed for him. Vincent wanted to marry her, but his family disapproved of the relationship. Theo took him away to the country. He settled with his parents in their new home in Nuenen, where he had a small studio in his room.

COUNTRY STUDIES

"Diggers, sowers, planters, male and female, they are what I draw continually. I have to observe and draw everything that belongs to country life." The compassion that Vincent felt for poor people as a preacher was now channeled into his art. When a local business man asked him to decorate his dining room, Vincent painted six scenes of farm workers, with dark colors to emphasize the reality of peasant life. He also copied drawings of working people by famous artists whom he admired. One was the French artist Jean-François Millet, well-known for his paintings of country scenes.

The Sower by Millet was often copied. Vincent had a version by Le Rat, shown left. Vincent's copy, right, emphasizes the flowing central figure. He was working hard to overcome an early difficulty in drawing feet and hands.

DRAWING PEOPLE AT WORK

Drawing people can be difficult because they may want to be able to recognize themselves from your picture! Avoid this by drawing people at work. Don't try to draw faces in any detail. Instead, look at the shapes made by the outline of the whole body. Drawing stick figures may help you to understand where the weight of the person is resting. Try a series of three-minute sketches. Draw quickly to catch the movement of the figure. Shading can help to add depth to your picture. Practice more detailed sketches of parts you find interesting or tricky.

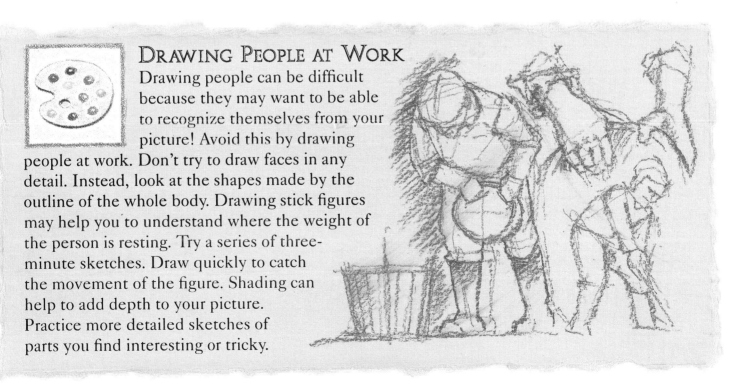

THE POTATO-EATERS

In 1885 Theodorus van Gogh died at his church in Nuenen, shown here. Vincent was shaken, but even more determined to succeed as an artist. His first major canvas, "The Potato-Eaters," summed up everything he had learned so far. By the end of the year he was ready to move on to new styles of painting in Antwerp and Paris.

A DUTCH TRADITION

"I propose to work on a canvas representing a group of country folk around a dish of potatoes, in the evening." Dutch painting is famous for interior scenes, and Vincent wanted to create a classic Dutch picture to bring him success as an artist. He constructed his painting with painstaking care over several months. He drew all the figures separately, sketching people he saw in the peasant homes he visited, and made at least 30 studies in oil. "I have such a feel of the thing that I can literally dream it," he wrote.

A MAJOR PICTURE

The Potato-Eaters was Vincent's most ambitious project so far. It was painted with a subdued palette of grays, greens, and browns, enlivened by yellow lamplight.

The faces are painted in a very realistic manner. At the time many artists painted romantic pictures of working people as young, happy, and beautiful. Vincent deliberately lit his peasants' faces to highlight their lined complexions and care-worn expressions. Even more remarkable are the gnarled and twisted hands poised over the bowl of glistening potatoes. He told Theo, "These people . . . have dug the earth with those same hands they put in the dish, having honestly earned their food."

Vincent's first major work was not well received. People disliked the dark colors, and found the worn faces of the peasants ugly. It was felt that the figures did not hold together as a group. As a result Vincent left the Netherlands for Antwerp and then Paris.

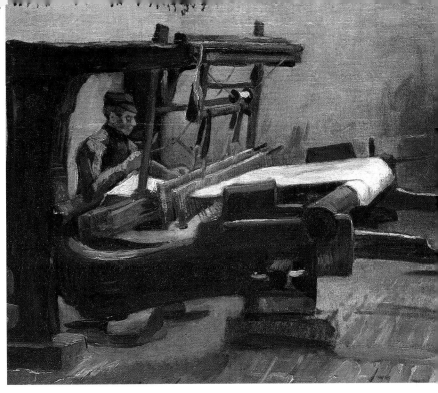

 The Weaver Facing Right, 1884. At Nuenen Vincent completed nine paintings of weavers.

The farmer's profile and cheek-bone catch the light cast from the right, but shade into darkness on the left. Many artists have used light for dramatic effect in this way. The term for the technique is *chiaroscuro*, which means "light-dark" in Italian.

◀ *The Potato-Eaters*, Vincent's first major canvas, was painted in April 1885.

LIGHT AND DARK

The objects you draw or paint will look real and solid on paper if you show the way light falls on them. Choose a round object like a ball or an orange and place it so that light falls on it from one side. Study how the light affects the colors of your subject and try to capture this in crayon or paint. If the light is shining from the right, you will need pale colors there, shading into dark on the opposite side.

Paris

Vincent spent two years in Paris, living near the hill of Montmartre with his brother Theo, who had become an art dealer. It was one of the most exciting times in the history of French painting. Through Theo, Vincent met many artists at the forefront of the new movement of "Impressionism." The impact on Vincent's dark, northern style was enormous.

The Impressionists

During his first exciting weeks in Paris, Vincent was much affected by the work of the Impressionist painters. He met many artists, including Paul Cézanne, Claude Monet and Camille Pissarro. These men and other artists spent hours discussing the future of art. Influenced by the Impressionists, Vincent abandoned the dark palette he had used for his northern paintings in favor of clear, bright colors. He began to paint street scenes with cafés like the one below, and parks with flowers.

Restaurant de la Sirène at Asnières, 1887. Vincent's colors have brightened dramatically.

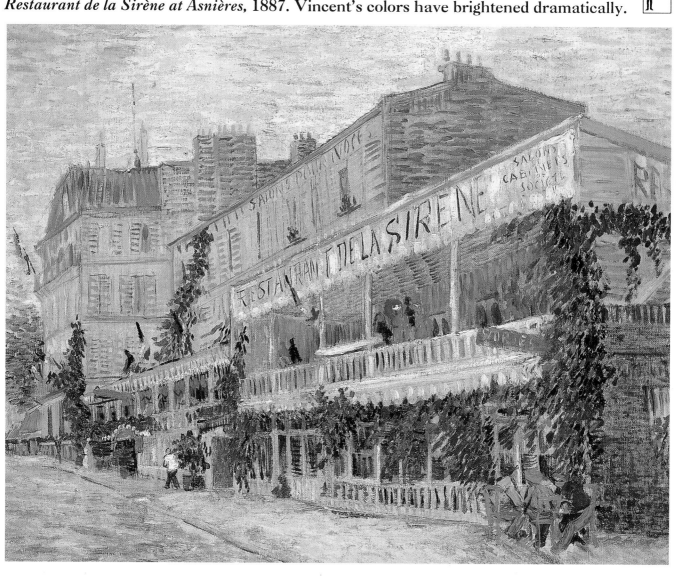

PAINTING SENSATIONS

The idea behind Impressionism was a bit like color photography. Impressionist artists believed that a painting should be a quick, excited response to a particular moment. They tried to express on canvas their "impressions" of the light and colors of a scene.

Vincent became friends with Paul Gauguin and Paul Signac, both young artists. Through Signac he became acquainted with the technique of Pointillism, a method of painting in dots of pure color (see below). For a while Vincent was influenced by the Pointillists. When he left Paris, the discoveries he had made about color and light stayed with him.

 *Interior of a Restaurant*, painted in 1887, was clearly influenced by Pointillist ideas.

HOME LIFE WITH THEO

Vincent was a difficult man to live with. Theo wrote to a friend: "No one wants to come and see me any more because it always ends in quarrels, and besides, he is so untidy that the room looks far from attractive. I wish he would go and live by himself." But Theo respected Vincent's intelligence and passionate heart, and their friendship survived.

POINTILLISM

The Pointillist movement was a development of Impressionism. Pointillist paintings are made up of small dots and touches of pure, bright color. From a distance the dots blur together to form other colors. Try a painting of your own in this style, using crayons, paints, or felt-tip pens. You could paint the view from your window, or try working from a photograph that interests you. Notice how mixing dots of certain colors makes other colors: a pattern of blue and yellow dots will look green, and so on. To find out more about how colors work together, see page 25.

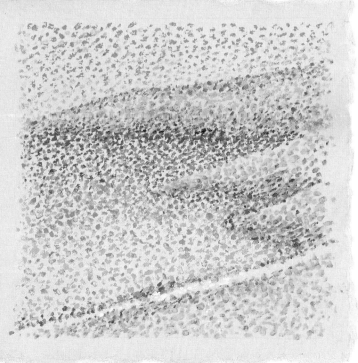

JAPANESE INFLUENCES

Paris and Impressionism had changed Vincent's painting, but he was still searching for a personal style. All through his life he was prepared to learn new ideas and techniques and use them in his own work. Toward the end of his stay in Paris, Japanese prints excited him and brought even more color and liveliness into his painting.

CAFÉ LIFE

Japanese prints were used as packing material around china imported from the Far East and were often thrown away afterwards. Vincent collected about 400 prints, and in the spring of 1887, a café owner named Agostina Segatori allowed him to put on an exhibition of them. In an age before radios, televisions, or telephones, street cafés were important places, lively with debates on politics and art.

Vincent showed his own pictures in a second exhibition, but he failed to sell any. He was becoming tired of Paris and yearned for a "place of retreat to get back one's tranquility and poise." Theo helped him to go to

Arles in the South of France. Arriving in February 1888, Vincent found the countryside covered in snow, "just like the winter landscapes that the Japanese have painted."

In the 1860s Japanese painting was popular. In May 1866 the magazine *Paris Illustré* featured this print by the artist Keisai Eisen. Vincent copied and enlarged it, using the technique of scaling up (see opposite page).

Vincent's version, *Japonaiserie: the courtesan after Keisai Eisen*, 1887 ▶

PÈRE TANGUY

"Father" Tanguy sold paints and canvas, and looked after artists when he could. He helped Vincent by storing hundreds of his pictures in an attic. Vincent has painted him surrounded by his favorite Japanese prints, including Keisai Eisen's figure, set against a different background. Vincent loved the simple colors and serenity of Japanese art. It made him think more about the design of a picture as a whole. His brush strokes were becoming much bolder and more confident. At the age of 34, Vincent was developing his own personal style of painting.

Portrait of Père Tanguy, 1887-88. Despite the confident style, the hands are awkward.

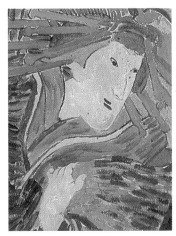

Japanese prints were very colorful. Because hundreds of each image were printed, they were used as decorations, as posters are today. They had simple designs, with flat areas of color, and strong outlines.

SCALING UP

Scaling up provides an easy way to copy a picture to a larger size. Vincent used this technique to make his copy of Keisai Eisen's picture. Cover the picture you want to copy with tracing paper and draw regular squares across it. Draw the same number of squares onto blank paper, but make the squares bigger if you want to enlarge the original. You can now copy each square of the original picture across to your own squares. Copy the outline first, making sure the edges of your squares match up. Then fill in the detail and the color.

ARLES

In Arles, Vincent found lodgings in a café, the Carrel (shown left). Local people were a little alarmed by the hoarse-voiced Dutch painter with red hair, and left him alone, but Vincent was delighted. He loved the landscape of the south, the light and the peace, and spent long hours painting in the fields and in orchards decked with spring blossoms.

SETTLING IN

In the late nineteenth century, the South of France was not fashionable and sophisticated, as it is today. Arles itself was a manufacturing town with an important railway and noisy modern streets outside the old town walls. Vincent wrote to Theo, "Although the people are blankly ignorant of painting in general, they are much more artistic than in the North in their own persons and their manner of life." He recovered from a bout of illness, and bought paints and canvas. He made friends with the local postman, Joseph Roulin (see page 23), and went with him to local cafés. Vincent was determined to make his home in Arles and wanted to establish a working group of artists around him there.

Entrance to the Public Gardens at Arles, 1888

LANDSCAPES

"Nature here is extraordinarily beautiful," Vincent wrote. He brought what he had learned in Paris about light and color to Arles, and these ideas were strengthened by the countryside. He walked for hours each day, setting up his easel and canvas in the open air, despite burning sunshine or biting wind. He wrote to his sister, "At present the palette is distinctly colorful – sky blue, orange, pink, vermilion, bright yellow, bright green, bright burgundy, violet."

He saw agricultural scenes that he knew from the Netherlands in a new light and repainted *The Sower* against an enormous yellow sun. The beauty of spring amazed him, and he painted the fruit trees in blossom, using a decorative approach drawn from Japanese art. He visited the coast where he painted picturesque fishing boats and made many trips to the canal near Arles, where there were bridges like those in the north. Inspired by these landscapes, his painting grew more confident, with powerful brush strokes and vibrant colors.

Pollard Willows and Setting Sun, 1888

Landscapes like the one shown above are full of energy. The grasses in the foreground are painted with confidence. The black lines of the branches criss cross the rays of the sun in a dramatic and expressive way.

USING OIL PAINT

Oils are completely different from any other kind of paint. Vincent used a paste of linseed oil mixed with ground-up pigments, colored powders made from natural substances such as rock. Today oil paints are rather expensive; you can achieve some of the same effects with cheaper acrylic paint. Some artists dilute oil paint with turpentine or white spirit to make it wet and smooth. Vincent used his paint thick, straight from the container.

Vincent brushed paint onto the canvas in thick, raised strokes (see detail below). The technical term for this is *impasto*. The strokes don't run together, as watercolor would, or let the color underneath show through.

Thanks to Theo, Vincent got his paints from a dealer in Paris. He was always asking for heavier, dryer paints, with purer colors, so that he could paint straight onto the canvas without any mixing or preparation.

SIMPLE GREATNESS

Vincent painted many of his greatest pictures in the summer of 1888, including his most famous painting of all, "Sunflowers." He began to experience fainting fits and stomach pains, but worked constantly, using up enormous quantities of paint that had to be sent to Arles from Paris. Theo was planning to marry, but still sent his brother money to live on every month.

 L'Arlésienne, 1888. The gloves and embroidered kerchief show Madame Ginoux to be a respectable woman.

NEW LODGINGS

From the Carrel café Vincent moved to new lodgings. He was eating too little and drinking too much, and was constantly anxious. He could be irritable with people, particularly when suffering from a toothache or stomach pains. Vincent was working at great speed. "One must strike while the iron is hot," he wrote. In 15 months he produced 200 paintings and many drawings. But sometimes he was "hopelessly absentminded and incapable of heaps of ordinary things." Poverty and too much hard work were making him ill. He felt at times elated, at times despairing, and began to fear for his own sanity.

A WOMAN OF ARLES

At his new lodgings, the landlady Madame Ginoux fed him well, and he slowly recovered. She allowed Vincent enough space to lay out his canvases to dry. She posed for her portrait in the local costume as a woman of Arles: *L'Arlésienne*. Vincent also painted the postman Roulin and members of his family. These portraits have a new simplicity, with the figures isolated against a background of pure color.

SUNFLOWERS

Vincent loved sunflowers, which became for him a symbol of the hot south, and painted them many times. *Fourteen sunflowers* was the fourth in a series of pictures painted in one week in August 1888. "I am trying to find a special brushwork without stippling or anything else, nothing but the varied stroke." In 1987 the painting was sold for £25 million. While he was alive, Vincent only sold one picture. He sent the others to Theo in Paris in return for his monthly allowance, and they were kept in an attic.

▲ *Fourteen sunflowers,* painted in 1888

◄ *Sunflowers (and one detail),* painted in 1888

STILL LIFE

A still life is a painting of everyday objects. Choose some objects and try them in different positions until you're happy with your composition, or arrangement. Study your subject and sketch the outlines in pencil. Then try to capture the colors and textures with crayons, colored pencils, or paint.

THE YELLOW HOUSE

In the summer of 1888 Vincent rented the wing of a house on Place Lamartine in Arles. It was painted yellow on the outside, and inside there was plenty of light to work by. Vincent saw it as a "house of friends" where other artists would come and stay. He bought furniture for it and had repairs done. It became a symbol of his search for peace of mind.

SETTLING IN

Vincent was pleased by his new home both inside and out, and did a series of paintings of the rooms. The colors of his bedroom delighted him, and he described them to Theo: "The ground is of red tiles. The wood of the bed and the chairs is the yellow of fresh butter, the sheets and pillows very light greenish lemon." Of his painting of this room (below) he wrote: "Color is to do every-thing . . . to be suggestive here of *rest* or of sleep. In a word, to look at the picture ought to rest the brain, or rather the imagination."

Vincent's bedroom at Arles, painted in 1889

GAUGUIN'S ARRIVAL

The artist Paul Gauguin, whom Vincent had met in Paris, was now living in the north. He was ill and depressed. Vincent promised him sun to help him recover his health, and the excitement of painting the southern land-scape. Gauguin arrived in October to a newly painted and furnished house. Gauguin's room was decorated with paintings of sunflowers and looked like the "boudoir of a really artistic woman." For the first six weeks of Gauguin's stay everything went well and the two artists painted together, learning from each other.

QUARRELS

Neither Vincent nor Gauguin had much money, although they went drinking in several bars. Soon it became obvious that their relationship was not going to be easy. Gauguin found Vincent untidy and emot-ional. But Gauguin himself could be over-bearing and very emphatic about his own ideas. He mocked Vincent for not painting from his imagination. Relations between the two grew strained, and they began to quarrel.

Joseph Roulin, **Vincent's friend the postman, painted in 1889**

PERSPECTIVE

Perspective makes a flat picture look three-dimen-sional. In your room, as in Vincent's, objects that are close look large, and those that are further away look smaller. The edges of regular shapes such as beds and walls seem to angle inward, to meet at a central "vanishing point," probably outside the room, as it is here. The skill is to get the same effect on paper. Try a drawing of your own room. Copy the angles of surfaces so that they recede in your draw-ing. You could pencil in lines radiating from a vanishing point first.

BREAKDOWN

By December 1888 there was considerable tension between Vincent and Gauguin. Vincent had experienced bouts of illness and hallucination, and these were becoming more frequent. In late December Vincent suffered a terrible mental crisis. He was taken to the hospital in Arles (shown left), where he had a complete breakdown. Yet within a month he was painting again.

CRISIS

Weakened by lack of nourishing food and exhausted by his work, Vincent had begun to lose control of his sanity. On the night of December 23, 1888, the crisis erupted. After supper Vincent threatened Gauguin, and Gauguin decided to spend the night in a hotel. Later Vincent became so distraught that he cut off part of his own ear. In the morning he was found unconscious in his bed.

Vincent was taken to the hospital, where he lay unconscious for three days. Theo rushed from Paris to visit him. In the hospital Vincent suffered another breakdown, but within a few days he seemed himself again. A priest from Arles who visited him wrote: "I found him chatting calmly and he did not appear to be at all deranged."

PAINTING AGAIN

Within a month, Vincent felt well enough to paint again. He wrote to Theo, now back in Paris: "I hope that what I had was only an artist's craze and a high fever because of all the blood I lost."

In January 1889 he returned to the Yellow House. Gauguin had left for Paris, and Vincent was alone and penniless. Later that month, his friend Roulin also left with his family, to live in Marseilles. Vincent's neighbors were frightened by the possibility of

Self-portrait, painted in 1889. Vincent's painting rhythm is preserved in the brush strokes.

further bouts of violent behavior. They wrote to the mayor requesting that Vincent be kept in the hospital. In February he was readmitted to Arles hospital, where he was taken care of by Dr. Rey.

This picture captures the attention partly because of its two main colors. Red and green are opposing or *complementary* colors (see below). They cause a moment of visual shock when put together like this.

Self-Portrait with Bandaged Ear and Pipe was painted in 1889.

SELF-PORTRAITS

In his life Vincent painted many self-portraits. Between 1885 and 1889 he completed over 40 pictures of himself in different moods: cheerful, professional, or miserable. In the self-portrait on the left, painted in 1889, Vincent looks grim and determined. The paint in the background is full of swirling energy. The lines continue down through the artist's jacket, making Vincent seem part of a tremendous force of nature.

The portrait above was painted in January 1889, less than a month after Vincent's first crisis. His ear was still bandaged, and the artist looks sad but dignified, puffing at his pipe. The brush strokes are very obvious in both works.

COLOR

Choice of color is a very personal thing, but there is also a theory of color that explains how different colors work together. The six basic colors on the color wheel shown here are divided into two groups. Red, yellow, and blue are the purest colors. They are known as *primary* colors. The *secondary* colors, green, orange, and purple, are mixed from the two colors on either side. Colors on opposite sides of the color wheel, such as blue and orange, are *complementary*. They intensify one another when placed together.

Experiment by mixing secondary colors from primary colors yourself. Notice how the pure colors merge together to form more complex hues.

Saint-Rémy

In May 1889 Vincent transferred himself from Arles Hospital to the nearby asylum at Saint-Rémy, where he spent a year. Theo arranged a bedroom and a studio, so that he could continue with his painting. There, between bouts of distress and illness, he seemed to recover, and carried on with his work.

At Work in the Asylum

Saint-Rémy was a converted monastery with its own grounds. In its well-regulated atmosphere, Vincent found he could work again. He painted trees and fountains, and the flowers of the garden (below). The doctors were sympathetic and allowed him out on painting trips. Between December 1888 and his death in July 1890, Vincent completed over 450 works. They are a record of his heroic efforts to continue the work he loved whenever he could. In the asylum he made paintings based on works by Millet, and copies of his own pictures such as his bedroom, painted in happier times.

Irises **was painted in the garden of the asylum in 1889.**

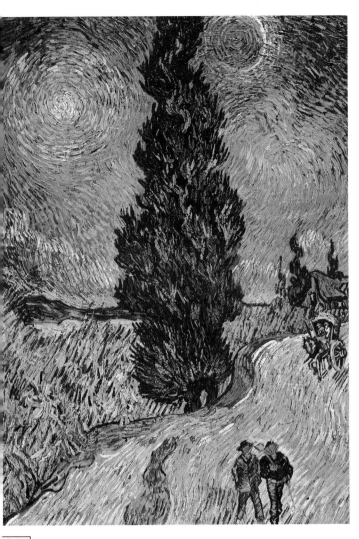

Vincent himself saw that his art and illness were connected. He agreed with Dr. Rey that "instead of eating enough at regular times, I kept myself going on coffee and alcohol ... but to attain the high yellow note I attained last summer, I need to be pretty well keyed up." On excursions from Saint-Rémy, Vincent produced a series of paintings of cypresses.

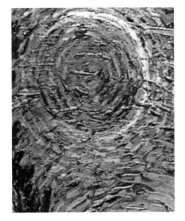

Thick strokes of paint create energy and drama. Each brush mark is alive with movement. The disturbing note struck by the tree is heightened by the strange night sky, with its blazing moon and star.

Vincent was astonished by the shape of cypress trees, like "Egyptian obelisks," and by their dark color, "a splash of black in a sunny landscape." Vincent's paintings at this time became even more animated, with swirling shapes.

Road with men walking, carriage, cypress, star, and crescent moon was painted in 1890.

COMPOSITION

Before beginning to paint, an artist must organize, or compose, the main shapes in the picture. The drawing on the right shows the composition of *Road with men walking, carriage, cypress, star, and crescent moon* in simplified form. Vincent's works had become more unusual in their composition. The diagonal line from bottom left to middle right makes it seem as though the road disappears into the distance. Whether you are painting a landscape, portrait, or still life, drawing simple shapes like these first will help to test if your composition works.

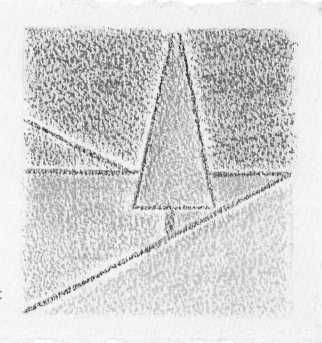

RETURN TO THE NORTH

In May 1890 Vincent left the asylum of Saint-Rémy for Paris. Theo had married and his wife was expecting a baby, and Vincent found that he missed the north. From Paris he moved on to Auvers-sur-Oise, an hour away. There he was looked after by Dr. Paul Gachet, a psychiatrist who was himself a part-time artist.

LIFE IN AUVERS

Vincent wrote to Theo of his new surroundings: "Auvers is very beautiful, amongst other things a lot of thatched roofs, which are getting rare." Without pausing to rest, he completed 70 canvases in as many days. These last pictures were turbulent landscapes, depicting vast fields under tormented skies (below).

The Wheatfield with Crows, 1890, a double-width landscape painted days before Vincent's death

However, Vincent's work was now putting an unbearable strain on his sanity. "My life is threatened at the very root, my steps are wavering." In an unfinished letter to Theo he wrote: "Well, my own work, I am risking my life for it and my reason has half foundered because of it." In the same letter he thanked Theo for his faithful support.

Doctor Gachet at a Table with a Sprig of Foxglove in His Hand, 1890

AN END AND A BEGINNING

After two months in Auvers, Vincent could stand the strain no longer. On July 27, 1890, at the age of 37, he went out into the fields and shot himself. He died two days later, in Theo's arms.

Vincent painted Dr. Gachet a month before he committed suicide. The doctor was interested in natural forms of medicine that made use of plants and herbs. Vincent painted him with a foxglove, the symbol of his trade.

After his death, Vincent's works were noticed and admired. Many artists were influenced by his bold style. Vincent did not suffer in vain. The paintings born of his anguish now bring happiness to people all over the world.

SYMBOLISM

The foxglove in the picture above is a flower, but it also stands for something else: it is a symbol of homeopathy, or alternative medicine. Here you can see some of the other symbols Vincent used in his pictures. What symbols would you use to represent yourself in your own drawings and paintings?

The sunflower represents ideas of the south, of sun and hope. It has also come to be a symbol for Vincent himself, because of his most famous picture.

The crucifix is a Christian symbol.

Books are a symbol of learning.

The flying crows that appear in some of Vincent's last landscapes have been seen as menacing symbols, representing the anguish of the artist's final, troubled months.

CHRONOLOGY OF VINCENT'S LIFE

March 1853 Vincent born.

October 1864 Sent to boarding school.

July 1869 Started work in The Hague branch of Goupil & Co., art dealers.

March 1873 Transferred to the London branch.

May 1875 Transferred to Paris.

January 1876 Dismissed by Goupil & Co.

April 1876 Arrived in Ramsgate to be an assistant in a school.

November 1876 Transferred to a school in Isleworth, West London.

January 1877 Studied to be a preacher.

October 1878 Failed his theology exams.

November 1878 Worked as a preacher in the Borinage.

July 1879 Fired by the church.

October 1880 Moved to Brussels to start learning to be an artist.

1881-1883 The Hague and Amsterdam.

September 1883 Lived in the Drenthe.

1884 Moved to his parents' house in Nuenen.

March 1885 Theodorus van Gogh died. In November Vincent went to Antwerp.

February 1886 Arrived in Paris.

February 1888 Arrived in Arles.

May 1888 Rented Yellow House in Arles.

October 1888 Gauguin arrived.

December 1888 Vincent had a breakdown and was taken to Arles Hospital.

May 1889 Moved to Saint Rémy.

May 1890 Arrived back in Paris, and later went to stay with Dr. Gachet in Auvers-sur-Oise.

July 1890 Shot himself in the fields and died two days later.

A BRIEF HISTORY OF ART

The world's earliest works of art are figurines dating from 30,000 B.C. Cave art developed from 16,000 B.C. In the Classical Age (500-400 B.C.) sculpture flourished in Ancient Greece.

The Renaissance period began in Italy in the 1300s and reached its height in the sixteenth century. Famous Italian artists include Giotto (ca.1266-1337), Leonardo da Vinci (1452-1519), Michelangelo Buonarroti (1475-1564), and Titian (ca.1487-1576).

In Europe during the fifteenth and sixteenth centuries Hieronymus Bosch (active 1480-1516), Albrecht Dürer (1471-1528), Pieter Breughel the Elder (1525-69), and El Greco (1541-1614) produced great art. Artists of the Baroque period include Peter Paul Rubens (1577-1640) and Rembrandt van Rijn (1606-69).

During the Romantic movement English artists J.M.W. Turner (1775-1851) and John Constable (1776-1837) produced wonderful landscapes. Francisco Goya (1746-1828) was a great Spanish portrait artist.

Impressionism began in France in the 1870s. Artists include Claude Monet (1840-1926), Camille Pissarro (1830-1903), and Edgar Degas (1834-1917). Post-impressionists include Paul Cézanne (1839-1906), Paul Gauguin (1848-1903), and **Vincent van Gogh** (1853-90).

The twentieth century has seen many movements in art. Piet Mondrian (1872-1944) painted in the Cubist tradition, Salvador Dali (1904-89) in the Surrealist. Pablo Picasso (1881-1973) was a prolific Spanish painter. More recently, Jackson Pollock (1912-56) and David Hockney (1937-) have achieved fame.

MUSEUMS AND GALLERIES

Some of van Gogh's works are in private collections around the world. However, most of his pictures, drawings, and letters were kept together and are now housed in a museum in Amsterdam especially devoted to his work, run by the National Vincent van Gogh Foundation.

Rijksmuseum: (National Museum) Vincent van Gogh, Amsterdam

The museums listed below have examples of van Gogh's work:

Courtauld Institute Galleries, London

The Metropolitan Museum of Art, New York

Musée d'Orsay, Paris

Musée Rodin, Paris

The Louvre, Paris

The Museum of Modern Art, New York

National Gallery, London

National Museum of Wales, Cardiff

Rijksmuseum Kröller-Müller, Otterlo

Stedelijk, Amsterdam

GLOSSARY

Chiaroscuro The use of light and shadow to make objects look real and three-dimensional in painting. The term means "light-dark" in Italian.

Complementary colors Colors that appear on opposite sides of the color wheel, such as red and green. Complementary colors intensify one another when placed side by side in a painting.

Impasto Oil paint applied in thick, raised strokes.

Impressionism An art movement that began in France in the 1870s. Impressionist artists aimed to capture an "impression" of light and color, rather than build up a very detailed picture of a scene.

Pigment Colored powders mostly mined from the ground, and mixed with various binding materials to make paint.

Pointillism A painting technique invented by the artist Georges Seurat and first seen in his painting *La Grande-Jatte*, which caused a sensation when first exhibited. This technique uses dots of pure color to build up an image.

Primary colors Pure red, yellow, and blue, the basic colors from which all other colors can be mixed.

Secondary colors Orange, green, and purple. The secondary colors are mixed from the primaries that appear on either side of them on the color wheel.

Still life A painting of inanimate objects such as fruit and flowers.

INDEX

INDEX OF PICTURES

Special thanks to: Vincent van Gogh Foundation/Van Gogh Museum, Amsterdam. Kröller-Müller State Museum, Otterlo. Bridgeman Art Library. Giraudin/Bridgeman Art Library. Frank Spooner Pictures. The publishers have made every effort to contact all the relevant copyright holders and apologize for any omissions that may have inadvertently been made.